BISHOP T.D. JAKES &

THE POTTER'S HOUSE MASS CHOIR

The Storm Is Over

ISBN 0-634-03869-9

HAL•LEONARD®
CORPORATION
7777 W. BLUEMOUND RD. P.O. BOX 13819 MILWAUKEE, WI 53213

Visit Hal Leonard Online at
www.halleonard.com

CONTENTS

LORD OF ALL

Words and Music by
JAMES THOMAS

Original key: E♭ major. This edition has been transposed down one half-step to be more playable.

Lord of all; _____ You are the might - y _____ King _____ of kings. _____

(See additional lyrics)

Additional Lyrics

Bridge: (Spoken, ad lib.:)
1. Let everything that hath breath praise ye the Lord!
Let's exalt His name together!
Let's rejoice before the King of kings, the mighty God, the everlasting Father.
Let every tongue and every nation, every culture and every kind rejoice before our God.
For there is absolutely no god like our God.
Let all the nations of the earth worship Him and adore Him.
Come on, Church, and lift Him up! He's worthy to be praised!

2. Every nation from India to Africa, from Germany to Australia,
From Jamaica to North America, let everything that hath breath praise ye the Lord,
And come before His presence with singing, with shouting and rejoicing.
For this is the day that the Lord hath made;
We shall rejoice and be glad in it!
Dance before Him!
(To Chorus)

Chorus: (Spoken ad lib. lyrics continue:)
Yes! Lift Him up!
There's nobody like Him! There's nobody like Him!
Can I get a witness?
You're the Lord of all!

He's wonderful! He's marvelous! He's my God! He's my King!
He's my bulwark, my trumpet, my strength, my life, my peace!
I don't know about you, but I will bless the name of God.
He won me! He taught me! He saved me! He led me out!
And I will bless Him. I can't help bless Him!
I got up to report, and I will lift Him up! Hallelujah!
(To Vamp)

Vamp: (Spoken ad lib. lyrics continue:)
Hallelujah! Hallelujah! Hallelujah!
Somebody wave your hands in His presence and just open your mouth and say "hallelujah"!

There's nobody like Him! He's in a class all by Himself!
I dare you to praise Him!

For Your blessings...for Your miracles...
For Your patience with me.... For Your kindness toward me...
I wanna say "hallelujah"!

For the trouble You brought me through,
For the place You're taking me to,
For the mountains we had to climb,
For the battles you pulled me out of,
Hallelujah!

BLESS THE LORD

Words and Music by
KEVIN BOND

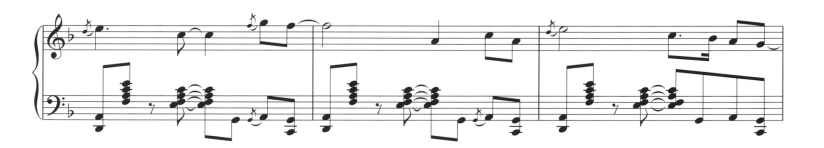

Bless the Lord, ___ oh, my soul, ___

THE STORM IS OVER NOW

Words and Music by
R. KELLY

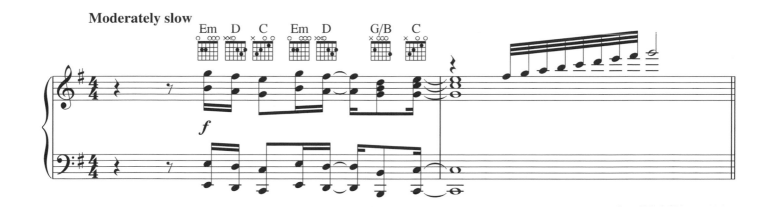

I tried to force a laugh, but my lips wouldn't lie. My heart was broken,
(Da, da, __ da.)

With pedal

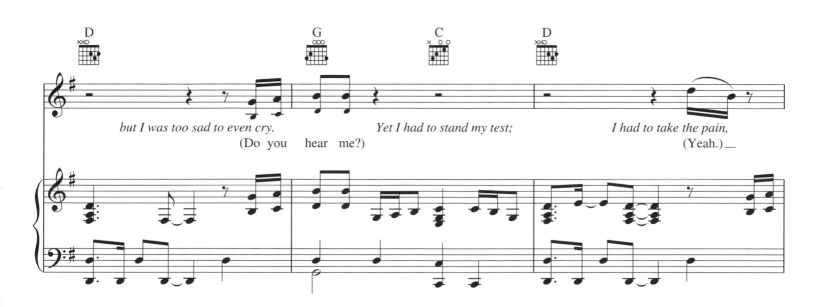

but I was too sad to even cry. Yet I had to stand my test; I had to take the pain,
(Do you hear me?) (Yeah.) __

WHEN MY SEASON COMES

Words and Music by
GUY ROBINSON

Original key: Gb major. This edition has been transposed down one half-step to be more playable.

LET YOUR GLORY FILL THIS PLACE

Words and Music by
GUY ROBINSON

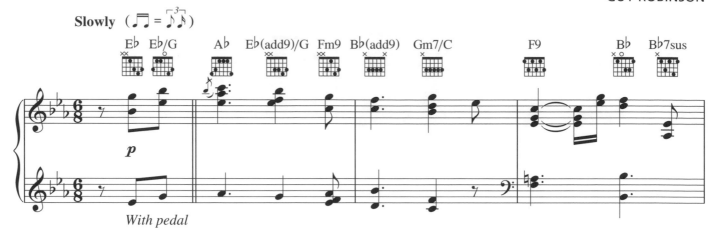

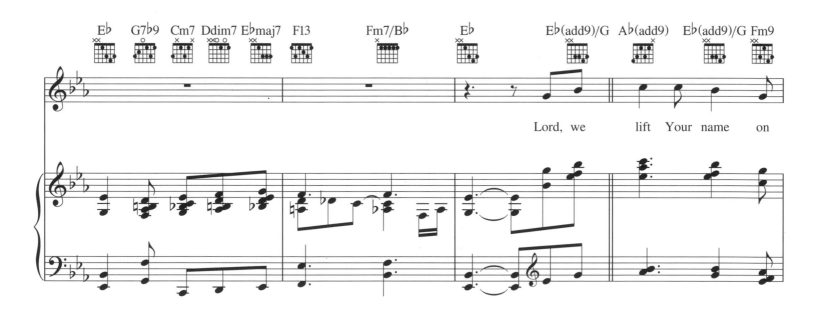

THOU ART MY HELP

Words and Music by
VINCENT SNEAD

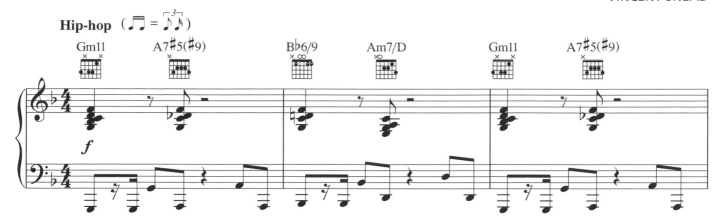

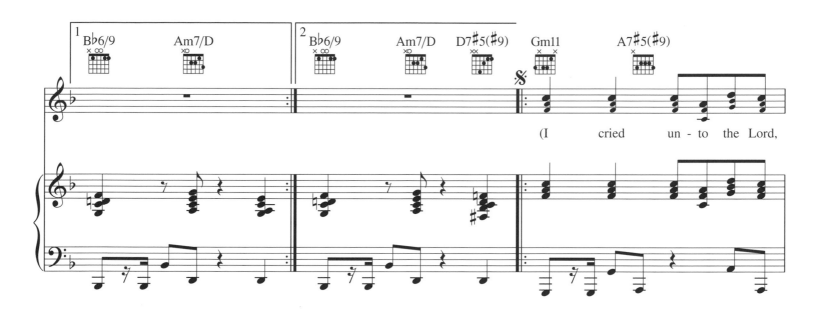

(I cried un-to the Lord,

and He pit - ied ev - 'ry groan.

Original key: Gb major. This edition has been transposed down one half-step to be more playable.

TRUST AND OBEY

Words by JOHN H. SAMMIS
Music by DANIEL B. TOWNER
Arranged by STEVE LAWRENCE

THE DEVIL'S ALREADY DEFEATED

Words and Music by STANLEY BROWN
and DANNY EVANS

Moderately fast, with a half-time feel

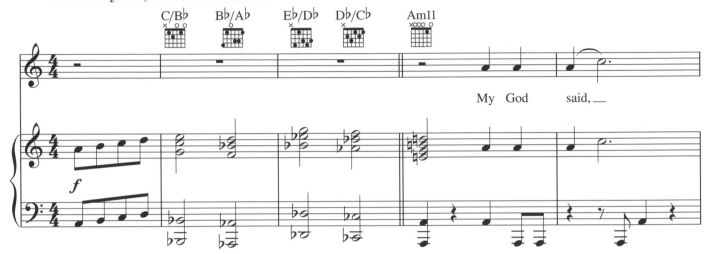

My God said, __

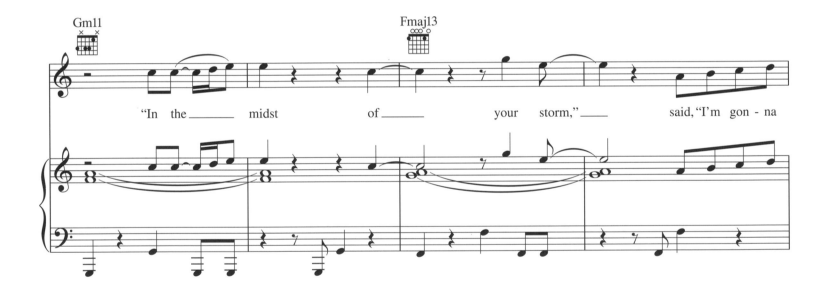

"In the ___ midst of ___ your storm," ___ said, "I'm gon - na

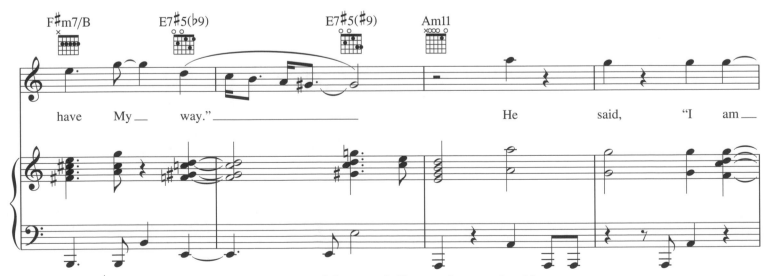

have My __ way." _____ He said, "I am __

Original key: B♭ minor. This edition has been transposed down one half-step to be more playable.

MARVELOUS

Words and Music by MYRON BUTLER
and TED WINN

Lyrics:
When I think of all the things
What the dev - il meant for bad, ____

that God ___ has taught me,
God used it to bless ___ me.

mar - vel - ous.
Mar - vel - ous.
(Mar - vel - ous in my ___ eyes.)

BORN AGAIN TO WIN

Words and Music by
KEITH CHILDRESS

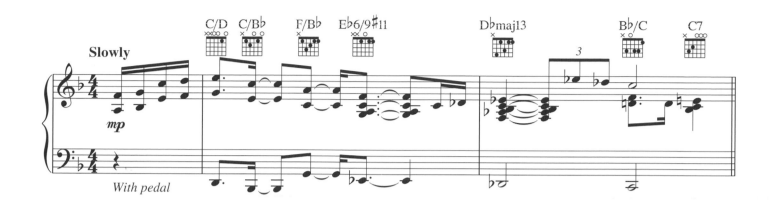

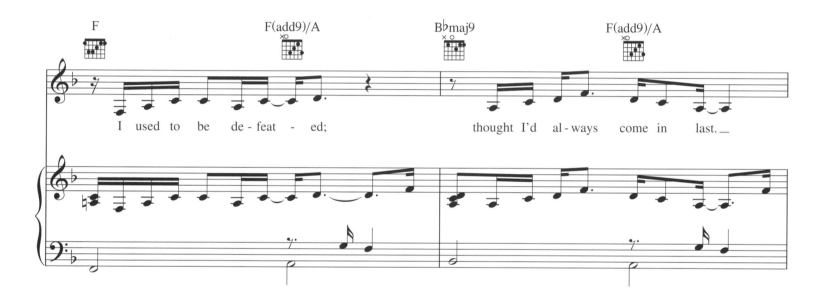

I used to be de-feat-ed; thought I'd al-ways come in last.

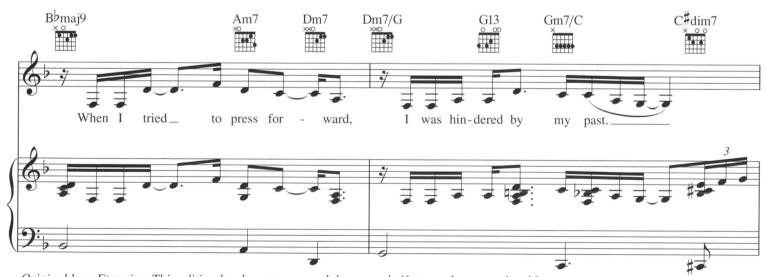

When I tried to press for-ward, I was hin-dered by my past.

Original key: F♯ major. This edition has been transposed down one half-step to be more playable.

nobody, nowhere, no time, no way. In all these things, we are more than conquerors.

Oh,_____ I've_ been born_ a-gain;_

_____ born a-gain_ to win.____ God's work has been com-plet-ed._ That old_

____ dev-il is de-feat-ed. No, nev-er a-gain_ will I ev-er be cheat-ed, I'm_

More Contemporary Christian Folios from Hal Leonard

AVALON – A MAZE OF GRACE

This matching folio includes: Adonai • Dreams I Dream for You • Forgive Forget • Knockin' on Heaven's Door • A Maze of Grace • The Move • Reason Enough • Speed of Light • Testify to Love • A World Away.

_____00306239 Piano/Vocal/Guitar $14.95

STEVEN CURTIS CHAPMAN – DECLARATION

13 songs: Bring It On • Carry You to Jesus • Declaration of Dependence • God Follower • God Is God • Jesus Is Life • Live Out Loud • Love Takes You In • Magnificent Obsession • No Greater Love • Savior • See the Glory • This Day • When Love Takes You In.

_____00306453 Piano/Vocal/Guitar $14.95

DC TALK – INTERMISSION: THE GREATEST HITS

17 of dc Talk's best: Between You and Me • Chance • Colored People • Consume Me • Hardway (Remix) • I Wish We'd All Been Ready • In the Light • Jesus Freak • Jesus Is Just Alright • Luv Is a Verb • Mind's Eye • My Will • Say the Words (Now) • Socially Acceptable • SugarCoat It • Supernatural • What If I Stumble.

_____00306414 Piano/Vocal/Guitar $14.95

DELIRIOUS? – SONGS FROM THE CUTTING EDGE

15 songs from this acclaimed 1998 double-disc release: All I Want Is You • Did You Feel the Mountains Tremble? • I Could Sing of Your Love Forever • I'm Not Ashamed • I've Found Jesus • Lord, You Have My Heart • Obsession • more.

_____00306243 Piano/Vocal/Guitar $17.95

JENNIFER KNAPP – LAY IT DOWN

All 10 songs from this 2000 release: All Consuming Fire • Diamond in the Rough • Into You • Lay It Down • A Little More • Peace • Usher Me Down • When Nothing Satisfies • You Answer Me • You Remain. Includes photos.

_____00306358 Piano/Vocal/Guitar $14.95

THE BEST OF SCOTT KRIPPAYNE

Features 10 songs: All My Days • Bright Star Blue Sky • Cross of Christ • Every Single Tear • Hope Has a Way • I Wanna Sing • No More Pretending • Sometimes He Calms the Storm • You Changed the World • You Have Been Good.

_____00306356 Piano/Vocal/Guitar $14.95

THE MARTINS – DREAM BIG

This matching folio includes 10 songs: Come On In • You Come to My Senses • Go Where the Love Flows • Be Strong • Dream Big • We Trust in God • Except for Grace • He'll Be Holdin' His Own • Count Your Blessing • More like a Whisper.

_____00306323 Piano/Vocal/Guitar $14.95

BABBIE MASON – NO BETTER PLACE

10 songs from this gospel diva: Change Me Now • Holy Spirit, You Are Welcome Here • The House That Love Built • I Will Be the One • Isn't That Just like God • Love to the Highest Power • Only God Can Heal • Pray On • Show Some Sign • Stay Up on the Wall.

_____00306357 Piano/Vocal/Guitar $14.95

STACIE ORRICO – GENUINE

This debut release from Orrico features 13 songs: Confidant • Dear Friend • Don't Look at Me • Everything • Genuine • Holdin' On • O.O Baby • Restore My Soul • Ride • So Pray • Stay True • With a Little Faith • Without Love.

_____00306417 Piano/Vocal/Guitar $14.95

THE BEST OF OUT OF EDEN

A great compilation of 13 hit songs: Come and Take My Hand • A Friend • Get to Heaven • Greater Love • If You Really Knew Me • Lookin' for Love • More Than You Know • River • Show Me • There Is a Love • and more.

_____00306381 Piano/Vocal/Guitar $14.95

TWILA PARIS – GREATEST HITS

This folio celebrates Twila's career with 18 hits: Destiny • Faithful Friend • God Is in Control • He Is Exalted • How Beautiful • Lamb of God • Sparks and Shadows • The Time Is Now • We Bow Down • We Will Glorify • and more.

_____00306449 Piano/Vocal/Guitar $14.95

JANET PASCHAL – SONGS FOR A LIFETIME

12 favorite songs: Another Soldier's Coming Home • Been Through Enough • The Body and Blood • Born Again • Faithful Father • God Is Up to Something • God Will Make a Way • I Am Not Ashamed • I Give You Jesus • If I'd Had My Way • My Soul Is Anchored to the Rock • Written in Red.

_____00306328 Piano/Vocal/Guitar $14.95

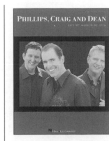

PHILLIPS, CRAIG AND DEAN – LET MY WORDS BE FEW

This 10-song collection includes: Come, Now Is the Time to Worship • How Great You Are • Let Everything That Has Breath • Let My Words Be Few • Open the Eyes of My Heart • You Are My King • Your Grace Still Amazes Me • and more.

_____00306437 Piano/Vocal/Guitar $14.95

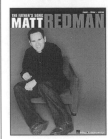

MATT REDMAN – THE FATHER'S SONG

Features 14 songs: The Father's Song • Holy Moment • Justice and Mercy • King of This Heart • Let My Words Be Few • Light of the World • Nothing Is Too Much • O Sacred King • Revelation • Take the World but Give Me Jesus • You Must Increase • more.

_____00306378 Piano/Vocal/Guitar $14.95

REBECCA ST. JAMES – TRANSFORM

Includes 12 songs: All Around Me • Don't Worry • In Me • Intro • For the Love of God • Lean On • My Hope • Reborn • Merciful • One • Stand • Universe • Wait for Me.

_____00306418 Piano/Vocal/Guitar $14.95

ZOEGIRL

11 terrific songs from this debut album: Anything Is Possible • Constantly • Give Me One Reason • I Believe • Little Did I Know • Live Life • Living for You • No You • Stop Right There • Suddenly • Upside Down.

_____00306455 Piano/Vocal/Guitar $14.95

FOR MORE INFORMATION, SEE YOUR LOCAL MUSIC DEALER, OR WRITE TO:

HAL•LEONARD®
CORPORATION
7777 W. BLUEMOUND RD. P.O. BOX 13819 MILWAUKEE, WI 53213

For a complete listing of the products we have available, Visit Hal Leonard online at **www.halleonard.com**

Prices, contents and availability subject to change without notice.

0302